# EDDIES
# for Outdoorsmen

Inspiration from Nature
and Outdoor Sports

by

Henry L. Youndt

**Eddies for Outdoorsmen:**
**Inspiration from Nature**
**and Outdoor Sports**
*by*
*Henry L. Youndt*
hyoundt@wjtl.net

Copyright © 2004

Library of Congress Number: 2003115953
International Standard Book Number: 1-930353-95-2

*Printed by*
Masthof Press
*219 Mill Road*
*Morgantown, PA 19543-9516*

# Contents

# Introduction

This book is a collection of short articles related to nature and outdoor recreation, especially canoeing, which is my favorite sport. Some of the articles were inspired by the intriguing beauties and marvels of nature. Some of them are the result of stupid mistakes I have made or lessons that I have learned the hard way. Some are the rambling thoughts of an outdoorsman. Others are fond memories of outdoor experiences I have had. But they are more than stories and facts.

I hope you will find here not only appreciation for nature, but appreciation for life. In addition to tips for safer canoeing, you will find tips for better living. Some articles will inspire you and some will leave you with questions to ponder.

We need to take time to smell the flowers and listen to the birds. We also need to listen to our hearts, check our compass and choose our destination. After reading each of these short articles, take a few minutes to reflect on your own life's experiences, let your mind wonder and listen to that little voice inside you. I do not have the answers to very many of life's issues, I can only prompt you to think about the issues. I hope this book will help you to enjoy the eddies you find along your way.

*- Henry L. Youndt*

# Eddies

I am somewhat of a white-water enthusiast. Although I prefer to stay away from the more dangerous water, I do enjoy working with the river currents to maneuver my boat around obstacles. As we white-water boaters navigate a river, we look for eddies. Down river from a rock or other obstacle there will be an eddy where the water is swirling and running upstream. The boater can drive his boat into a suitable eddy and with the help of the currents he can quickly turn the boat around and stop, facing upstream. Here in the eddy the boater can rest and relax while the water rushes by on all sides. Here he can pause and enjoy the beauty of the river. Here he can standby while fellow boaters test their skills in the rapids. From here he can study the river and plan his next maneuvers.

On one canoe trip I recall coming upon a pair of canoeists standing knee deep in rushing water, struggling desperately with a swamped canoe. About ten yards downstream from them was a small eddy from a submerged rock. I spun my canoe into the eddy and stopped. The eddy was so small it was virtually hidden by my sixteen-foot boat, but it was strong enough to do the job. It must have looked as though some mystical power was holding my boat in position against the current. As the men in front of me struggled to pull their boat from the raging current, I sat quietly in my canoe, using the handle end of my paddle as a hook to retrieve their gear as it floated by. One of the pair looked at me in amazement and exclaimed, "How in the world are you doing that?"

Eddy turns are a skill that every white-water enthusiast should master, not only for the sake of safety, but in order to enjoy the river to its fullest. On the river of life we also need to find the eddies. All of us need to find some quiet time when we can rest and relax as the world rushes by on all sides. We need time to observe our situation, reflect on the past and plan for the future. Where can we find these eddies? Naturally, vacations can be a time of rest and relaxation. But we also need to stop in the smaller, more frequent eddies. A supervisor I once worked for had a forty-five minute commute to and from work each day. He said he liked having that time alone to reflect on the day's events and plan for the next day. Things like jogging or walking the dog can provide us with eddies. Many religious people set aside a time each day for meditation and prayer. Making good use of the eddies on the river of life will help us cope with life's difficulties, maintain our sanity and enjoy life to the fullest. Are you finding enough eddies along your way?

# Mountain-top Memories

Mountain tops seem to be favorite places to enjoy the beauty of the world around us. With the sounds of civilization so far in the distance, even the quiet whisper of a gentle breeze seems loud. The air is fresh and clean. Everything seems so serene and peaceful. Buildings and cars are miniaturized. Maybe it's here that we see things in their proper perspective. The blue sky and warm sunshine can make our worries and cares evaporate. Suddenly we're free to relax and enjoy what mother nature has put here for us, a hawk soaring gracefully below us, a chipmunk eyeing us cautiously from a distance, a rattlesnake sunning himself on a rock. We take time to examine the wild flowers. We look at the trees and wonder how old they are. We look at the rocks and ask, "How did they get here?" We could linger for hours just gazing into the distance.

But we can't stay here forever. So what can we take with us? No, not the chipmunk, not the rocks or even the wild flowers. We want to leave it all for others to enjoy. However, there is plenty we can take from experiences like this. In fact, in some way we will probably take all of it with us.

# First Steps of a Fawn

When our two children were preschoolers, my wife and I began taking them along on backpacking trips. Once the four of us joined my brother Dean for a few days on the Loyalsock Trail in northern Pennsylvania. We started in Worlds End State Park and hiked to Route 220.

As we were plodding along one day, Dean stopped in his tracks and said softly, "I smell deer." All of us stopped and gazed intently around us as we sniffed the air. I was not familiar with the smell of deer, but I could easily detect an odor similar to that of horses. After surveying the area for some time we spied a newborn fawn lying in the leaves by a tree stump not far from the trail. His natural camouflage made him very difficult to see as he lay there quietly watching us. If we had not stopped and looked carefully over the area we would have completely missed this wonderful experience.

Although we stood there for some time peering into every nook of the forest around us, we never got a glimpse of his mother. I'm sure she was hiding somewhere nearby with her ears perked up, anxiously waiting for us to leave so she could rejoin her fawn. Eventually the little fellow got to his feet, perhaps for the first time, and walked slowly away from us. We turned and continued on our trail. Although we left him there, we carry him in our memory forever.

There is something about baby animals that makes us want to pick them up and cuddle them. Maybe it's because they seem so helpless and vulnerable in a wild and hostile environment. We usually give birth to our babies in a sterile environment with the assistance of medical professionals and modern equipment. Perhaps we tend to overlook the miracle that takes place at childbirth. Sometimes we forget how much longer it takes for our own offspring to get to their feet and take those first steps. If it is the helplessness of these little ones that brings out the tenderness in us, then our own infants should be the most loved and cared for of all species. Most of the time, I suppose that is the case.

# Sledding Adventures

From the front of the house where I grew up you could look up at a hill that provided some of the best sled runs I have known. There were a lot of different routes you could take with a variety of slopes and distances. The steepest slope was along the edge of one field right by the woods. This area was almost too steep for operating farm equipment. In fact it was too steep, but the farmers did it anyway. About a hundred yards down the slope there was a fence row running horizontally along the hillside. Over the years this row of trees and brush had built up a natural terrace by capturing topsoil that eroded from the slope above. So at the fence row the ground leveled out for a few yards then dropped almost vertically about five feet. Below the fence row the hillside continued at a more gradual slope. Obviously, mother nature had designed this area to give young boys the most thrilling sled ride possible. At just the right place in the fence row there was an opening plenty wide enough to guide a sled through without hitting anything big.

One at a time, we would lie on our sleds and speed down the hill headfirst, aiming at the opening between the trees. We would hit the ramp that nature had provided and fly into the air. The impact of the landing felt somewhat like being kicked in the stomach. I don't know why we thought that was fun. I don't know why we thought we could do something like that without killing ourselves. I guess the fact is, we just didn't think.

Sometime in my late teen years I returned to this slope for another exciting ride. I gave no thought to how much I had grown since the last time I had done this. I hopped on the sled and flew down the hill and into the air. I braced for the landing. Crack! Both handles broke off the sled, my fists plunged into the snow and I slammed my face into the sled. My contact with the ground ripped me off the sled which continued down the hill without me. I was a bit shaken but not seriously injured.

This painful incident may have been the first real evidence that I was growing up, or at least that I was getting heavier. Sooner or later all of us need to recognize that we're not kids anymore. It's time to leave childhood things behind and begin accepting the responsibilities of adults. Some of us may require a certain amount of pain or broken bones to help us learn that lesson. Some of us may never learn.

But for those who have learned, life should still be an enjoyable adventure. Things like choosing a vocation, getting married, buying a house, and raising children are adult adventures. They require us to venture into the unknown with a certain amount of faith and self-confidence. Sometimes we may get hurt. But if we keep our lives on the right track, we are likely to survive just as well as we survived our childhood.

# Bail Water or Sink

My first canoe camping experience was a trip on the upper Delaware. My friends Manny and Sam invited me and my brother Dean for a few days of paddling through this beautiful area.

As we approached the area known as The Hawk's Nest, we could see a series of large waves. I got out my movie camera and filmed Manny and Sam as they rode majestically over the waves. Then they pulled to the side and I gave the camera to Manny so he could film Dean and me doing the same.

Being amateurs, we did what most amateurs do. We paddled hard and gathered speed as we approached the waves. Our bow plowed into the first wave and buckets of water spilt over the gunnels adding fifty pounds or more to our load. There was no time for bailing. The waves were one right after the other. So we carried the extra weight with us into the second wave. More buckets of water poured into our canoe. Now we carried even more weight as we plunged into the third wave.

With each successive wave our boat sank deeper and deeper into the water till the only part that could be seen was a small deck plate at the tip of the bow. Dean and I sat in water up to our waists as we paddled toward shore and directly toward our friends with the movie camera, who seemed to be enjoying the experience more than we were. As soon as the bow of our submerged canoe struck the shore, the current flipped it over and we went for the swim we so much deserved.

I've done a lot of canoeing since that and I can't count the times that waves have spilt over my gunnels. When this happens I have a choice. I can carry the extra weight with me or I can bail it out at my earliest opportunity. I don't need to tell you which is the smartest thing to do. Carrying the extra weight slows my progress and causes me to work harder. It also puts me at greater risk when passing through turbulent water. But sometimes I just don't feel like bothering with that little bit of water sloshing around in the bottom of my boat.

Sometimes we carry with us the weight of anger and resentment from past experiences. This emotional baggage makes it more difficult for us to cope with the problems we face day by day. It may cause us to experience even more anger. If we continue to carry these feelings with us they may eventually overwhelm us. We may become suicidal, violent or dependent on drugs. Medical science tells us that negative emotions like anger, jealousy and resentment effect how our bodies produce hormones. Hormones control the functions of our organs. So negative emotions can make us ill, or weaken our immune system so that other things can make us ill. Bitterness and resentment can destroy us. When we forgive others we do ourselves a really big favor.

Are you carrying any water in your canoe?

# Death Spiral

My friend Dale and I once owned a 16 foot fiberglass boat on which we mounted a 75-hp outboard motor. The engine was certainly too big for the boat, but we had lots of fun with it. We discovered that the hull was designed in a way that allowed us to turn sharply at full throttle. When we did this the stern would skip over the water like a stone, and if you were sitting in the back seat you had to hang on tight.

Once while I was water skiing, Dale started the boat into a gradual turn. I started pulling to the outside of the turn and picking up speed. Then he pushed the throttle all the way forward and turned hard. Soon I was cruising like a missile. The problem was I was skiing on trick skis, which have no fins on the bottom. At high speeds these short curved skis just skim the surface with only a small portion of the ski actually touching the water. This gives the skier virtually no control at all. The only way I could maintain any control was to keep cutting in with the edges of the skis. That meant I had to keep pulling to the outside of the turn which made me go even faster. If I leveled out my skis, centrifugal force would pull my feet out from under me and I would fall toward the boat. The centrifugal force of my body pulling against the rope was so great that if I released the rope the recoil would send me for a loop. The only thing I could think of doing was to keep the edges of my skis cutting in and hang on with all my might until my friend either slowed down or stopped turning. He did neither. Faster and faster I went till my arms could no longer stand the strain. I went flying! My skis went flying! I tumbled over the surface of the water for quite a distance before I plowed under in a huge splash.

In life there are many death spirals much more dangerous than my little skiing incident. Things like gambling, credit card debt, and drug addiction can put us in a position where we think our only hope is to continue doing the very thing that is destroying us. In these situations, people need the help of others to get their lives back under control. Tragically, many people don't receive that help before they have a devastating fall.

# Song of the Wood Thrush

On warm summer evenings, my wife and I love to sit outside and listen to the wood thrushes singing in the woods behind our house. Their sweet flute-like calls with various trilled endings are relaxing and interesting to listen to. It gives me the impression that they must be contented and happy, although I really don't know why they sing like that. Maybe they are to inspire us to use our voices to the fullest potential. Just think about the wide variety of sounds our voices can produce. Consider all the vowel sounds and consonants that we can combine to create an endless variety of words. We attach meaning to these words and use them to communicate ideas and emotions. We use tone and inflection to convey much more than the meaning of the words. We can arrange words to create poetic rhyme and meter. Consider the range of pitches we can use to create countless melodies. Think about our ability to blend our voices in harmony with others. It seems to me that anybody who has been given a human voice should not be at all impressed by the voice of a wood thrush. But I still like to hear them sing.

# Solo or Tandem

Both solo and tandem paddling are lots of fun and each have their own rewards. I enjoy the freedom of paddling solo and being fully in charge of my own canoe. Of course, when something goes wrong I have no one to blame but myself. The solo paddler may get a little extra satisfaction out of guiding his boat through a narrow channel without scraping a rock, or running difficult rapids without capsizing. He may feel more self-sufficient than a tandem paddler, but he also has to work harder to get from point A to point B.

Tandem paddling is more efficient and so requires less energy than paddling solo, provided the pair has learned to work together. It can also be a very exhausting and frustrating experience for those who do not know how to work as a team. There are some inherent difficulties for two people operating one canoe. The person in the bow naturally has the best view of what lies ahead and is in the best position to spot those rocks which always pop up at the last second. However the person in the stern has much greater control of the boat. There are steering strokes that the bow paddler should be familiar with, but the stern paddler is responsible for most of the steering. It is also difficult for the person in the bow to give verbal instructions to the person behind him. Unless he turns and faces backwards, his voice will go out over the water where often there is nothing to bounce the sound back to the stern paddler. If the pair are not aware of these problems or do not know how to cope with them, they will likely begin blaming each other.

I always enjoy having my son in the bow. I know I can depend on him to spot the obstacles and choose a good course. He knows the correct steering strokes to use and has the strength to use them effectively. When I see the direction he is steering, I respond appropriately. Not a word is needed. Oftentimes I can't see the obstacle we're steering around, I just follow his lead. I trust his judgment and rely on his strength. When each one is willing and able to do more than his share, the work load is greatly reduced.

Tandem paddling requires the same kind of teamwork that is needed for a good marriage. It requires trust and commitment. If one partner does not do his part, if one assumes too much control, or if they are unable to communicate effectively, the couple may end up on the rocks. In marriage and in canoeing there is great pleasure for the couple who learn to work together.

# Camping Stuff

Why would intelligent people in a modern society want to leave their comfortable homes and camp out in the wilderness? Why would they leave their cars and travel on foot or by canoe or horseback? I don't know, but I do know what fun it is. I know it can be enjoyable in spite of the hardships.

On one of our earlier backpacking experiences, my wife and I and our two children were using a lightweight nylon tent we had recently purchased. Someone had advised us to use a piece of plastic as a ground cloth to provide extra protection from the damp ground. I used a piece of plastic a little larger than the tent. I didn't see a problem with that. My ground cloth extended out several inches from the tent on all four sides. I never thought about what would happen if it rained. That night it didn't rain. It poured! All the water that ran off the tent collected in a pool under the tent. The plastic that was supposed to be keeping us dry was making us wet, very wet. Bigger is not always better.

In fact, when it comes to camping gear, smaller is often better. Less is better than more. Any camping trip requires planning and decisions on what to take and what not to take. You want to be sure to take everything you really need. But you don't want to be burdened with a lot of things you could do without. Too many things can be just as much, or more, of a problem than not having some things you would like, especially if you're carrying everything on your back.

If you are traveling by canoe or horseback, you don't have to be quite as weight conscious as a backpacker. But still, the more stuff you take, the bigger the tasks of setting up camp, tearing down camp and re-packing. After several days of unpacking and re-packing, you start to ask yourself, "Do I really need all this stuff?" After all, what is our goal? Are we trying to see how much gear we can drag into the wilderness, or do we want to see what we can survive without? Let's not allow our things to prevent us from really enjoying the wilderness.

At home, as well as in the wilderness, the over abundance of things can burden us down and stifle our enjoyment of life. First, we have the cost of purchasing all our gadgets. Then, we have to maintain them, find a place to store them, and pay insurance in case we lose them. Finally, we pay the garbage man to haul them away. Every once in awhile we should look around our homes and ask, "Do I really need all this stuff?" Of course, the best time to do that would be whenever you start thinking about buying more stuff.

# Pileated Woodpeckers

What a pleasure it is to observe the creatures of the forest in their natural habitat, especially those that tend to be a bit more shy, like the pileated woodpecker. This large, crow-sized woodpecker is mostly black with white markings. It has a slender neck and a red crest on the back of its head, which seems to extend the lines of its large beak, making the head look like a narrow triangle. The neck and head, which remind me of a small tomahawk, give the bird a rather fearsome appearance.

While strolling through the woods one day, I discovered the large, somewhat rectangular, hole of a pileated woodpecker high up in a dead tree. I watched and waited quietly. After about a half hour I heard the loud call of a pileated woodpecker as one came flying to the tree. Its mate immediately left the nest and vanished into the forest. The new arrival quickly disappeared into the nest.

A week or two later I returned with my camera and telephoto lens, hoping to get a shot or two of these elusive woodpeckers. I climbed up a steep hillside across from the woodpecker's nest and waited. Eventually one of the birds flew in and perched on the tree trunk just below the hole. To my surprise two little heads popped out. The adult began feeding the young and I began snapping pictures. It was all over in few seconds and the adult was gone. Although my pictures were not fantastic, it was quite exciting to capture these tender moments of this fierce-looking but timid bird.

*Awesome is just the right word*
*For such a magnificent bird.*
*The crown on his head*
*Of plumage so red*
*Is fearsome and graceful concurred.*

# Ring-necked Pheasants

When I was a boy, whenever my dad would go out small-game hunting he would almost always bring home several ring-necked pheasants. My brothers and I admired their striking colors: the bright red velvety patch around the eye, the iridescent green head, the bold white neck ring. As if that wasn't enough, the individual feathers covering the rest of the body had intricate designs in soft brown and russet colors. These are truly beautiful birds, and good eating too.

By the time I was old enough to hunt, ring-necked pheasants had become a bit more scarce. However, I had more than a few opportunities to shoot at them. The problem was that I wasn't fast enough or accurate enough with a shotgun. I don't regret it though, when I see how scarce they are today.

A neighbor of ours used to raise pheasants to sell to the Game Commission. Sometimes, when he needed an extra hand, he would hire my brother and me to help care for the pheasants. Unlike the chickens we tended at home, these birds had a wild nature. We always had to be careful not to alarm them. A sudden movement or noise would cause several of them to fly up, hit the wire fencing, and return to the ground. Their flight would frighten others into doing the same. They would fly up and return to the ground, look around and see others flying, then repeat it all over again. The chaos would go on and on. The only thing we could do was stand perfectly still till it was over. Many times when it was over, several pheasants had lost their lives by crashing into the fence.

Sometimes people react like pheasants. Someone suggests there is a shortage of a particular product and lots of us rush out to buy it. Demand goes up and the supply goes down. So more of us rush out to buy the product and the cycle continues. Or a group of investors believes that stock prices are about to fall, so they put their stocks on the market, pushing prices downward. Other investors see the prices falling and decide to sell. The downward spiral continues. Sometimes it takes a lot of courage not to react in panic. Incidentally, courage is one of those commodities in short supply. I think I'll rush out and buy some more.

# Hypothermia

One of the dangers of canoeing, and many other outdoor activities, is hypothermia. This is a condition when the temperature inside the central body drops below the normal 98.6 degrees Fahrenheit. Our bodies are designed, not only with a will to survive, but with automatic responses that help to preserve life as long as possible. As the core body temperature begins to drop, the person begins to shiver uncontrollably. This helps the muscles to generate more heat. At around 95 degrees the heart rate slows down and the blood pressure begins to drop. Breathing and all other body functions slow down as well. Although this allows the surface of the body to get much colder, it also reduces heat loss from the core where the vital organs are located. While this increases the length of time the person can survive, it also decreases his ability to rescue himself. His thinking becomes cloudy and as the temperature reaches about 93 degrees he loses manual dexterity as his muscles become rigid. Between 90 and 86 degrees the victim usually becomes unconscious. As the temperature of the brain decreases, the brain's need for oxygen also decreases. At low temperatures the brain can endure long periods with no blood flow and suffer little or no brain damage.

It may be possible to resuscitate a victim even after there are no signs of life. Organizations like the Red Cross and the Coast Guard can provide you with plenty of information on first aid for hypothermia. If you haven't already, take time to learn how to treat this dangerous condition.

Plan your outdoor activities in a way to avoid the risk of hypothermia. Dress in layers and wear clothes that will keep you warm even when wet. When boating on cold water, take extra clothes in a watertight container. Remember, any alcohol in your blood stream will increase your risk of hypothermia. While alcohol makes you feel warmer, it is actually cooling you and decreasing your chances of survival.

Our bodies are equipped with some wonderful tools for survival—the greatest of these is common sense.

*Camper canoe invented by the author.*

# Invent Something for the Fun of It

In the early 1970s, my friend Manny and I started taking canoe camping trips on the upper Delaware River. At first it was easy to find places to camp along the river. Over the years the area became more and more populated, with no trespassing signs, till it became almost impossible to camp anywhere but in a commercial campground. I am one that likes to get away from the crowds and camp in seclusion, so this problem bothered me.

Eventually, I came up with an idea. What if I could camp right on the water? I came up with a plan to build a canoe that could be converted into a camper, somewhat like a miniature houseboat. When open, it would be large enough to sleep four adults. When closed it would be a standard-size canoe.

Almost as soon as I had come up with the concept, my thinking began to shift from camping and fun to making money and getting rich. Maybe this invention was my ticket to an easier lifestyle. I documented my idea and went to see a patent attorney.

I am so thankful that this attorney brought me down to earth. He told me the idea of making money from an invention is almost a fairy tale. A large majority of inventors lose money on their inventions. He encouraged me to build one for my own use and document my work in case I decide later to apply for a patent. So I did that.

I bought a used canoe and cut it in half along the keel line. I made each half into an individual pontoon. The two halves can be drawn together with a system of nylon ropes threaded through pulleys located near the keel line. The halves can also be spread apart a distance of about four feet. There is a sheet of rubberized fabric permanently attached to the two hull sections just above the ropes and pulleys. When the hulls are spread apart, this fabric stretches out on the surface of the water, creating a large water bed. The ends of the fabric curve upward at the bow and stern to keep the water outside. Aluminum poles are inserted into sockets to support a tent-like cover over the top. It works pretty well.

If you've got an idea, I encourage you to build on it. Record your work by taking pictures and keeping a journal. Although in the end I decided not to patent my invention, I have no regrets about building it. It was fun, educational and interesting every step of the way. Who knows, maybe your idea will be more profitable than mine. But don't let the prospect of wealth ruin the joy of being creative and the fun of experimenting and building. Most of all, if you have any dreams about getting rich, be very cautious. There are plenty of people and businesses out there who are eager to exploit your dreams and relieve you of all the money you are willing to invest.

# Manual Power

I lean forward, plant my paddle and pull it back propelling my canoe forward. By adjusting the curve of my stroke I can turn left or right. The canoe is really a simple vessel. It has no complex engine burning fuel to generate power, and no complicated steering system. It has no sophisticated navigational equipment, no communication equipment, no electrical system and no computer. On the other hand, you could say that a canoe uses all the above.

A canoe utilizes the most complex and sophisticated propulsion and guidance system ever designed, the human body. Carbohydrates fuel the system of muscles that generate the power to move and steer the boat. The eyes and ears gather information about surrounding conditions. The inner ear supplies information regarding balance. The eyes, ears, mouth and even the hands work at communications. Inside the body a network of nerves carry electrical and chemical signals that control the muscles and send information to the brain. The brain is constantly processing the information from the rest of the body, storing data and sending out instructions.

The human body is truly marvelous and superbly designed. Long before man discovered electricity, electronic signals were flowing through our bodies. Long before we figured out how to build a capacitor, our hearts were being zapped by rhythmic electrical pulses. Long before man ever dreamed of a computer, our brains were doing what no computer has ever done, thinking creatively.

# Venus' Flytrap

The Venus' flytrap is a unique plant that grows in the coastal region of North and South Carolina. It can grow in boggy areas where the soil lacks important nutrients because it gets these nutrients from insects it traps in its leaves. The upper portion of each leaf is made up of a pair of lobes hinged to a center rib. These lobes, fringed with sharp bristles, form the jaws of the trap. The inner surface of each lobe has three sensitive hairs. When an insect disturbs one of these hairs the trap closes quickly with the spiny bristles around the edges interlocking. Special glands in the leaf produce enzymes which digest the insect. After the insect has been digested the lobes reopen to await another victim.

According to the theory of evolution these unique characteristics developed gradually over millions of years as slight mutations changed the plant little by little. Mutations which benefited the plant helped it survive and were passed on to following generations, while those that did not benefit the species died out. This is called the process of natural selection or survival of the fittest.

But wait a minute, the Venus' flytrap would have had to develop to a degree of perfection where it could successfully trap an insect before these mutations would have provided any benefit to the plant. Almost catching a fly would not have supplied any nutrition whatsoever to the plant. It seems to me that these unusual characteristics should have died out long before the species captured its first insect. Also a system for digesting the insect had to be developed in order for the plant to benefit from that first successful capture. For these unusual features to continue developing before there were any benefits to the plant would require planning based on future benefits. That requires intelligence. The plant doesn't have a brain.

My conclusion is that this species was designed and brought into existence by a highly intelligent being. What else might such an intelligent being be responsible for?

# Blueprint for the Universe

Look around at all the different things you see. Look at all the different kinds of trees, with different types of leaves and unique types of wood. Consider the thousands of species of other plants, each with their own special make up. Consider how many different kinds of rocks and minerals there are on this earth. Think about the hundreds of thousands of species of insects that inhabit the earth. And don't forget about all the different birds, mammals, reptiles and fish, each one a complex body made of many different materials.

All of this, from the air we breath to the ground we walk on, is composed of only 103 basic elements. The atoms of these 103 elements are made up of three types of subatomic particles; electrons, protons, and neutrons.

Scientists have discovered that these 103 elements are organized in groups that can be shown on a chart called the periodic table. The elements are placed on the chart in order by the number of protons in the nucleus of each atom. They are placed in horizontal rows according to the number of layers or *shells* of electrons orbiting the nucleus. When arranged in this way the elements in each vertical column have similar characteristics in regard to how they react with other elements. This chart holds the key to how everything works, from living things to the formation of rocks, from electronics to the unique characteristics of water.

The basic elements from which our world and its ecosystems are built are so organized that it is hard for me to believe they are the result of a random explosion. To me, the periodic table suggests order and planning. It is easier for me to believe that this was planned by an Almighty Creator than to believe that it all came about at random. I don't understand the Big Bang Theory at all. If everything started with a big explosion, what exploded? Where did it come from?

# A Guiding Star

I am not much of an astronomer, but I enjoy looking up at all the billions of stars on a clear night. The number of stars, their size and distance from us is beyond my comprehension. I can only identify three constellations by memory—the Big Dipper, Little Dipper, and Orion, the hunter. I will usually check to see if I can still find them. They are always right where they are supposed to be, although sometimes I may be a bit confused.

For centuries sailors and explorers have used the stars to find directions and determine their location. Probably the star most used for this is the North Star. Because the North Star is located on the axis of the earth's rotation, it does not rise and set as other celestial bodies do. All during the night the North Star appears at the same place over the northern horizon while the other stars appear to move in a circle around it.

Is it mere coincidence that a star is located on the axis of our earth's rotation? Is it coincidence that this star is the proper brightness and distance from Earth so that it can easily be seen with the naked eye? Is it also coincidence that it appears to be directly in line with the two bright stars in the end of the Big Dipper, where even I can easily find it? Is it coincidence that this star is located over the hemisphere where civilization first began and where man first set out to explore the lands and seas around him? I prefer to believe that all the stars were put in their places by the almighty creator. The North Star suggests to me that this Creator God cares about sailors, explorers and other outdoorsmen just like me.

# Dependable Trade Winds

Sailing ships have always fascinated me. They make magnificent pictures as they cut through the water with their white sails billowing out from a maze of ropes and spars. As a boy I read stories about ships, drew pictures of them, and built models of them. I wondered what it would be like to climb the rigging to the topgallant mast of a clipper ship, then creep out onto the yardarm and furl the skysail. I have never done such a thing and I'm not sure that I would want to. The fascination continues, however.

Equally fascinating are the trade winds that drove these mighty ships. For centuries sailors have depended on these winds to get them to and from their destinations. Wind direction was even more important before sailors learned how to tack their ships into the wind.

As the sun warms the air over the ocean, the warm air rises and is replaced by heavier air which is being pushed out from the poles by centrifugal force. Since the poles are the center of the earth's rotation, the air coming out from the poles is moving eastward more slowly than things closer to the equator. Therefore, this air curves to the west as it moves toward the equator. I suppose this pattern will continue as long as the earth turns and the sun shines.

I wonder how differently our civilization would have developed if these trade winds did not exist.

*Canoes rigged for sailing in the Allagash wilderness.*

# Sailing Canoes

Soon after we started paddling on Eagle Lake in Maine, we stopped by a thick pine forest. Typical of the area, this forest was so thick that small dead trees were in abundance. We found four logs about three inches in diameter and cut them to ten feet long. We put our three canoes side by side, laid two of the logs across and lashed it all together to form a raft. We lashed the other two logs together at right angles to form a mast and yard-arm. We erected the mast in the center of the middle canoe and hoisted a tarp as a sail.

The light breeze caught our sail and sped us along our way. Using our paddles only as rudders, we soon made up for the time we spent building this primitive looking, but efficient, watercraft. We finished our day much farther ahead than we would have been if we had not utilized the power of the wind.

For centuries men have used the wind to drive ships and turn windmills. Ever since long before that mother nature has been using the wind to spread pollen and carry plant seeds. Winds carry the moisture from the lakes and oceans to the mountains and plains. Winds help to distribute the sun's heat, which is what creates the wind in the first place. Some species of birds use rising air currents to keep them aloft without flapping their wings.

I sincerely thank the One who created a world with moving air currents.

# Solar Eclipse

An eclipse of the sun is always a fascinating occurrence. As the shadow of the moon sweeps across the earth, we experience a short period of darkness. Birds may react as if it were evening and settle into their nests only to be aroused a few minutes later as the sun reappears. In ancient times, man had some strange beliefs about the cause of this strange phenomenon. The Chinese believed a dragon was trying to swallow the sun. A total solar eclipse gives scientists a rare opportunity to study the sun. Because the moon is just the right size and distance from earth, it can completely block out the sun but still leave visible the layer of thin gases known as the corona.

Is it mere coincidence that the moon is just the right size and distance from earth to provide man with an opportunity to study the sun? Or is it evidence that the Creator knew that man would be interested in studying the universe around him?

# Like a Diamond in the Sky

While watching for the international space station to pass overhead, I noticed an unusually bright object in the sky. I could detect a variety of colors as it twinkled through the haze. At first I thought it might be a distant airplane coming directly toward me so that I was seeing both red and green navigation lights along with strobe lights and beacons all in one cluster. That was not the case, however. Through further observation and research I realized this was the Dog Star, Sirius, the brightest star in our sky, excluding the sun. According to the *World Book Encyclopedia*, Sirius radiates thirty times as much light as the sun. The light I was seeing was actually generated almost nine years earlier. Since that time it had been traveling through space at a speed of 186,282 miles per second. What a distance that light had come. Sirius is actually one of the stars closest to our solar system. The vastness of the universe just boggles my mind.

# The Thirsty Moon

Isn't it lovely to watch a bright full moon rise slowly over the horizon? The soft light of the moon seems to have some sort of romantic influence on us. The moon has been an inspiration to lovers, poets, astronomers and scientists.

If you could, would you want to visit the moon? I'm not so sure that I would. Why would I want to travel a quarter million miles to a place that has no fishing, no swimming, and no canoeing? I think the greatest experience on the moon would be looking up into the black sky and seeing the big shining earth with blue oceans and white clouds full of that wonderful stuff called water.

Why is it that seventy percent of the earth is covered with water and the moon has none? Maybe it's because the moon doesn't need any. Mars and Venus, our next closest neighbors, have very little water compared to Earth. It is this vast amount of water on earth that keeps the temperatures from going to the extremes that occur on other planets. Water makes the earth a very unique place. No wonder the moon keeps tugging at Earth's water.

When the big bang happened, and everything that didn't exist exploded and created the universe, how did so much water end up on the earth and so little on earth's neighbors?

*Leftover relics turning to rust in the wilderness.*

# Allagash Dinosaurs

Deep in the Allagash Wilderness in Maine there are two dinosaurs. They can be found in a narrow strip of woodland between Chamberlain Lake and Eagle Lake. Well, they're not actual dinosaurs. They are two 90-ton steam locomotives, leftover relics from a previous era when lumber barons were making fortunes by stripping this land of its virgin timber. When these machines became obsolete they were left behind, along with a lot of other junk, to turn to rust in the wilderness.

Mother nature is reclaiming her territory, however. Plants and wildlife are flourishing in this area that was once overrun by the logging industry. Today we manage our forests, and timber is growing back faster than it is being cut. If we let nature take its course, trees will eventually cover almost any landscape. With a little care and management we can provide ourselves with a constant supply of timber and pulp wood and at the same time provide a habitat for wildlife. You don't have to be a radical to work with mother nature. She gave us common sense. Let's use it for her benefit.

# A World Without Weeds

When the weather is dry and the lawns turn brown, shrubbery dies and crops wither; but, it seems, the weeds remain green and healthy. Keeping weeds out of gardens and flower beds can be a never-ending task. These hardy plants are able to survive the tough conditions with no cultivation and propagate themselves with no assistance. Did you ever wonder what it would be like if weeds did not exist?

There would be much more soil erosion, for one thing. Any land that is not planted in crops would become barren and the rain would wash it away. Good topsoil would become very scarce. Wild animals would lose their habitat. Plant-eating animals would have to rely on man's crops for food. Without weeds, much of the animal kingdom would perish.

Weeds help to prevent soil erosion and put humus back into the soil. They provide food and habitat for wildlife. We all need these nuisance plants that survive almost anywhere, under almost any conditions. We just don't need them in our gardens.

# A Tree for Every Purpose

Raise both of your arms till they extend straight out from your shoulders. How long can you hold them like that? Now look at a tree. Notice how much longer the branches are than your arms. Think about how heavy the branches are compared to your arms and how far out that weight is from the tree trunk. Think about the constant stress that occurs where the branch connects to the trunk. Think about the added stress when the wind blows or snow falls. The tree holds its branches out there, not only a few minutes, but hour after hour, day after day, year after year. Through sun and wind and rain and snow the tree never rests. If the branches were made of steel, they would probably fatigue and break. But they are made of an amazing material called wood.

Although wood is quite strong, it is light enough to float on water. It does not fatigue from stress and flexing, as many metals do. Most species are soft enough that nails and screws can easily be driven into them. Some species, such as hickory and hard maple, are very hard and excellent for making durable tool handles and hardwood floors. Many species, such as cherry and walnut, are desirable for furniture and cabinetry because of their beautiful colors and grain character. Teak contains oil that makes it resistant to water and so it is used on boats and ships. Species like ash and mahogany have excellent strength-to-weight ratios. I've seen an ad claiming that marine grade mahogany has the best strength-to-weight ratio of any building material known to man. Redwood and cedar have a high resistance to rot and insect damage. Various types of wood are used for making expensive guitars, violins and other musical instruments. For every purpose there seems to be a wood species designed to meet the need. Wood has a moderate degree of insulating quality. It can also be burned as fuel or processed into other products such as paper and plastic. I believe wood is truly the most versatile and easy-to-use raw material known to man. How convenient it is that this amazing material grows naturally in the wild.

You may put your arms down now.

# Stone Cutting

For most of my life my vocation has been in the wood-working industry. However, I have found a lot of enjoyment in some small home projects working with stone. My woodland has sandstone everywhere, stones wedged one against the other. Stones are easier to find than soil. Sometimes I wonder how anything can grow here. But whenever I want to build something, I don't need to buy stone.

I'm not sure why I find this rugged work so enjoyable. Maybe it's the much needed workout I get swinging a twelve-pound hammer and carrying or tumbling heavy stones from place to place. Maybe it's the feeling of power I get from splitting a large rock into manageable pieces. Maybe it's the sense of accomplishment I get by dressing and shaping the stones with a three-pound hammer and a chisel. Maybe it's pride in building something my friends will admire. Maybe it's the feeling of significance from knowing that my project will be here longer than I will. It's probably all the above. But more than anything, I believe it's the satisfaction of making something useful from raw materials which I've taken directly from the earth. I thank God for creating rocks and putting them on this beautiful planet for our use.

*Water cascading over rock layers at Spruce Lake Retreat in the Pocono Mountains of Pa.* Sketched by the author.

# Panorama
# Based on Rocks

There is a scenic area in the lower Susquehanna where I like to spend a few leisurely hours paddling my canoe among the massive rock formations. Over the years the river has carved these rock layers into a group of islands holding enough soil to support a variety of trees and wild flowers. As I wind my way through narrow channels I gaze in awe at the high rock walls around me. I am fascinated with the changing scenery as I quietly slip in and out of the little coves. I enjoy watching the birds and admire the wild flowers, but it's the rocks that really amaze me.

How long did it take for all these rocks to form? How long did it take for the river to wear them away? I don't know. Geologists tell us that as these rock layers are wearing away new ones are being formed. Sediment packs together and slowly hardens into a layer of rock. Some existing rocks are slowly changing from one type into another. For example, some limestone is gradually changing into marble. If the hardness of the rocks is continually changing, then it seems we could be way off on our estimates of how long it took for these channels to be carved out. Looking at all the erosion on the rocks here in the Susquehanna, one might think it would have taken millions of years. However, if the river started washing away the material before it was completely hardened, the erosion would have been much faster.

There are many places which are bigger and more spectacular than this little area in the Susquehanna. The Grand Canyon is probably the biggest and most well known. Many of these places have some mind-stretching estimates of their age. I have to wonder if the geologists making those estimates considered the fact that those thick layers of rock were at one time nothing more than packed sand.

Rocks are the foundation of our landscape. They form the mountains and the plains, the river beds and ocean bottoms. Without rocks we wouldn't have streams and rivers to generate power and use for transportation and recreation. Not only do they shape our landscape, but they add interest and beauty as well. There is hardly a fern or flower whose beauty is not enhanced when placed on a rock ledge or in front of a stone wall. Now add a reflective pool of water and a blue sky to the picture. Then think to yourself, "What a wonderful world!"

# Gentle Robins

Have you ever watched robins pulling worms out of the ground? Sometimes they appear to be pulling with all their strength. However, I am convinced that they are really not pulling very hard at all. Earthworms are very tender and can be torn in two very easily. The robins are simply using the same technique that I used when I collected worms to use for bait.

When I was a youngster, my brothers and I would occasionally go out after dark to collect night crawlers. Often when we tried to pick up a worm, we would discover that one end of it was securely anchored in a hole in the ground. If you pulled just a little too hard the worm would tear apart and you would have only a small piece of it. But if you pulled gently and kept the worm stretched for a few seconds, it would soon become tired and relax its grip on the hole. Then you could pull the entire worm out of the hole.

I have noticed that robins also seem to be quite skilled in getting whole worms out of worm holes. I suppose it is even more difficult for them to get an entire worm, since they are gripping them with sharp beaks rather than soft fingers. If they bite down just a little too hard they will cut the worm in two and lose the part in the ground. Somehow they have learned that being gentle pays off.

# Campfire Reflections

    Almost all of us outdoor enthusiasts enjoy sitting around a campfire. Even if we don't need a fire to keep us warm, even if we're not roasting hot dogs or toasting marshmallows, we still gather around the fire. We sit in a circle gazing at the campfire and let our worries drift away with the smoke. Next time you're gazing into one of those fires think about this.

    The fire is just releasing the sun's energy which the trees stored up years earlier. The tree leaves use the energy from sunlight to combine carbon dioxide and water to make carbohydrates which become part of the wood. The excess oxygen is released into the air. Now as the wood burns, oxygen from the air combines with the carbon and hydrogen in the wood, energy is released in the form of heat and light, and the carbon dioxide and water rise into the air.

    We and other members of the animal kingdom do the same thing the fire does. We get energy by burning the carbohydrates we have taken in as food. We inhale oxygen and exhale carbon dioxide. The plant kingdom takes our carbon dioxide and gives us back oxygen and carbohydrates. There are also other ways that these two kingdoms depend on each other and provide for each other. I suppose this relationship will continue so long as we both shall live.

    But, how did it begin? I find it hard to believe that both of these kingdoms developed randomly from a single life form. How could these early life forms have known that the supply of either carbon dioxide or oxygen would eventually become depleted if they did not develop in opposite ways?

# Dancing Pebbles

Sometimes it doesn't take much to fascinate me. I've entertained myself by watching the sunlight play over a bed of colorful pebbles under a few inches of rippling water. The sparkling clear water made the pebbles shine. The light rays refracting through the waves cast moving highlights over the pebbles and made them appear to dance in the sunlight. The show was as good as any kaleidoscope and even provided a few interesting photographs. Light is interesting.

Light rays have waves of various frequencies. Since different surfaces reflect different frequencies while absorbing the others, we have a world of color. So light not only helps us find our way around the planet, but fills us with awe at the beauty of our surroundings. However, light has an even more important function. Because it can travel through the vacuum of outer space, it carries the sun's energy to earth. This not only warms the earth but provides the energy for photosynthesis in the leaves of plants. Plants provide us with food and oxygen. In other words, without light, life would be totally impossible. No wonder God created light on the first day of creation.

*Canoes crossing the Allagash Lake in Maine.*

# Wonderful World of Water

Why did the Creator cover more than two-thirds of the earth with water? I suppose it was because He knew how much fun it is to go canoeing, sailing, water skiing, snorkeling, fishing, cliff diving, surfing, swimming, and splashing in puddles.

Water is the most common substance in our environment. *World Book Encyclopedia* says there are about 326 million cubic miles of water on the earth. Yet it is also one of the most unusual substances on earth.

Water is the only substance which occurs naturally in all three forms, solid, liquid, and gas. Because water can change from liquid to gas and back to liquid again within the temperature range of the atmosphere, we have an endless supply of fresh water. Only about 3% of the water on earth is fresh. However, as water evaporates from the oceans and returns to the earth as rain or snow, the supply is continually replenished.

Water also has an unusually high heat capacity. In other words, water can absorb a large amount of heat without becoming much warmer itself. Without this characteristic of water our summers would be much hotter and our winters much colder.

Like all other substances, water contracts as it gets cooler and expands as it gets warmer. However, when water cools to below 39 degrees Fahrenheit it begins to do just the opposite. It expands as it gets cooler. If it were not for this unique feature, our lakes, oceans and rivers would freeze from the bottom upward. As a result, they would probably freeze solid. Think about the devastating effects that would cause.

Without all these unique properties of water, life as we know it could not exist on earth. All those water sports are just a bonus.

# Enchanting Clouds

When I take outdoor photographs I usually like to have a blue sky with some puffy white clouds. They give the picture a fresh clean flavor. Not only do clouds help make photos interesting, but they are relaxing to watch as they drift through the sky, continually changing their shapes. As a youngster, I recall lying on the lawn with some friends, watching large cumulous clouds and looking for recognizable shapes. Once we saw the distinctive face of George Washington. But his face soon became distorted and disappeared as the cloud billowed upward.

Clouds shade us from the intense heat of the sun and help filter out some of the sun's harmful radiation. It is always fascinating to look down on the clouds from the window of an airplane or from a mountain peak. Life above the clouds is always sunny. But, how quickly these puffy white clouds can change into dark, angry storm clouds. Although they appear light and fluffy, they can drop thousands of tons of water on the earth. One inch of rain on one square mile equals over 72,500 tons of water. What would we do if we could just control those little white monsters that float around in the sky? History suggests that the first thing we would do is use them in warfare against our enemies. I guess we're better off just letting it up to God to send rain on the righteous and the unrighteous.

# Lost Treasures

When I was growing up, one of the most interesting pets we had was a raccoon named Rascal. Whenever we brought him into the house we had to keep him under constant surveillance. Left on his own, he would go into the kitchen and directly to the bread drawer. He would pull the drawer open, grab a loaf of bread and run for a hiding place.

Once we gave him an ice cube. He took it to his water dish, put it in the water and fondled it as raccoons often do with their food. As he did this, the ice kept slipping out of his paws. Each time he lost the ice he would feel around his dish till he retrieved it, then he would continue "washing" it. Of course, the ice kept getting smaller and smaller till finally there was nothing left. For quite some time he continued feeling around his dish, trying to find his lost treasure.

I suppose we all have had some treasure that slipped through our fingers and disappeared. Maybe it was a collection of baseball cards that you lost track of, or some shares of stock that you sold at the wrong time. I had a '56 Chevy that I sold for a hundred dollars. I wonder what that car would be worth today. But life goes on. I don't want to be like that raccoon, trying to retrieve something that is no longer there.

# Key to Success

My son and I were canoeing with a group of fathers and sons on the upper Delaware River. When we started out in the morning, it was a bit cool so I wore a pair of jeans over my swimming trunks. Later, as the sun beat down on the river, I decided it was time to remove a layer of clothes. As we drifted with the current, I slipped out of my jeans. While I was doing this I heard something fall from my pocket into the water. I thought about what I had in my pocket, just a nickel and a quarter. There was no cause for concern. I could easily afford to lose thirty cents. As I went about stowing my pants it dawned on me that the splash I heard was too big for just a nickel and a quarter. What else did I have in my pocket? Oh no! My car keys!

The water was two to three feet deep and crystal clear. But I didn't know exactly where I had dropped my keys. As we turned our boat around, I called out to the boats following us, informing them of my dilemma. As we circled back over the area I envisioned calling my wife late Sunday afternoon and giving her directions for a four-hour drive to bring me a spare set of keys. This was not a pleasant thought. The other boats drifted over the area, everyone peering into the water. Suddenly a boy in the last boat yelled, "There they are, Dad! I see them!" His dad didn't ask where. He just said, "Well, jump in and get them." The young fellow jumped into the water and came up with my keys. I am forever grateful.

Some opportunities in life are like that. You don't have
time to sit and discuss it. You can't wait for a better opportunity.
You can't afford to let it slip away. You just have to dive in and
grab it.

# Priceless Beauty

Everyone knows how beautiful a sunset can be. But how often do we take time to really appreciate it? When did you last take time to watch the slowly changing colors from beginning to end? Psalm 19 says, "The heavens declare the glory of God; the skies proclaim the work of His hands." Each sunset is unique. There are no reruns. Artists and photographers may capture them on canvas or on film, but they can never reproduce all the splendor of a single sunset. They may sell their reproductions and impressions for a high price, but the original sunset is free for anyone who will take time to look. The original will be enjoyed only by those who take the time to appreciate it while it is there. The premier showing is the final showing. As the sun sinks below the horizon, the brilliant colors begin to dim, the sky gradually darkens and the show is over. What a lovely way for the Creator to say goodnight.

# Finding
# Physical Evidence

Strolling along a stream one day, my son and I found a stone arrowhead. For me it was a rare find. I am not one to go looking for such things, although I have stumbled onto a few old coins while working in the fields. Such artifacts are not only interesting novelties, but they provide an important link to the past. They give us physical evidence to support what we have learned about history, or they may shed new light on history. Fossils and dinosaur bones give us evidence of animals we have never seen. Archaeology in the Mideast provides plenty of evidence that the Bible is historically accurate.

In 1947 a shepherd boy discovered some old scrolls in a cave. This was the first of what became known as the Dead Sea scrolls. They include the oldest known manuscripts of parts of the Bible. These old manuscripts are almost identical to those which were copied by hand many times over. It is very unusual for a work of literature to have so few changes after being copied so many times over so many years. Obviously, the Jewish scribes who copied and recopied this book believed they were copying something sacred, not to be modified or embellished in any way. I am convinced that is exactly what they were copying.

# Paper Making

What did hornets use to build their nests before paper was invented? *World Book Encyclopedia* states that paper was invented by the Chinese around 105 AD. It has gone through centuries of development and improvement to become the product we know today. The availability of paper has had an over-whelming impact on modern civilization. However, mankind was not the first to make and use paper. Wasps and hornets were making paper thousands of years before the Chinese learned how to do it. Some say it was by studying these paper-making insects that the Chinese first developed a process for making paper. Hornets and wasps don't send their young to trade school or put them through an apprenticeship program. It seems they already have this knowledge when they hatch. Just as I can buy a computer with software already installed, their tiny brains are pre-programmed for making paper. Some species make open single-layered nests while others make enclosed multi-layered nests. They don't think about why they do it. They don't look for better methods or copy designs from their neighbors. They simply behave the way they are programmed to behave. The question is, "Who wrote the program?"

# Yellow Jackets and Honeybees

While working in the yard one day, I noticed some sweet-smelling flowers my wife had planted. Dozens of honeybees and bumblebees along with a variety of butterflies were gathering nectar from the flowers. On the ground, hidden among the stems, was an opening to an underground yellow jacket nest. Hundreds of yellow jackets came and went, paying no attention to the flowers that attracted so many other insects. They passed right by this wonderful food supply at their doorstep and flew long distances to feed on garbage.

I suppose the reason they did this was that a yellow jacket's mouth is not designed for sucking nectar from flowers. Their mouths are designed for biting and chewing. They didn't really have much choice.

I, on the other hand, have plenty of choices in regard to how I feed my body and how I feed my soul. How often do I pass up what is best and go out of my way to feed on garbage?

# Habits of the Honeybee

Honeybees are interesting little creatures because of their highly efficient work habits and their fascinating social life. They navigate by one of the same methods sailors use, called *dead reckoning*. That is, they determine the distance they must travel and the direction. Honeybees define their direction by using the angle of the sun. When one worker bee finds a food source she returns to the hive and does a little dance. Through this dance she communicates to the other workers the heading and distance to the food. I have heard that before each bee leaves the hive she eats just enough to give her the amount of energy required to fly the distance to the food source.

It is interesting to me that creatures so precise and efficient will continue to work at storing food when they already have stored far more than they will need. Why not kick back and take it easy? Perhaps the Creator programmed them that way so that they will have plenty to share with you and me and an occasional black bear. That's a thought that I really appreciate when I have a stack of pancakes in front of me.

# To Fly Like a Vulture

Behind my house there is a narrow strip of woodland running east and west. When the wind blows from the north or south, I often see vultures gliding along just above the tree tops. They are surfing on an invisible wave created by the air flowing perpendicular to the tree line. How they find this invisible wave I do not know. Do they know when it will be there and when it won't? I don't know. I know they have a unique ability to find the air currents which will give them a lift. You can often see groups of them soaring in circles. A common misconception is that they are circling over a dead carcass. The truth is that they have found a thermal, an upward spiraling column of warmer air. They instinctively use these thermals to gain altitude as they glide along effortlessly and gracefully. Although the vultures appear rather grotesque on closer view, it is relaxing to watch them soaring so smoothly and quietly through the sky. These birds also provide a valuable scavenger service.

Man has long desired to fly like the birds. We have built all kinds of flying machines, from jumbo jets to hang gliders, from helicopters to sail planes. Yet they are all clumsy, noisy or inefficient when compared to a vulture. No human flight instructor or aircraft designer can compare to the One who created vultures and taught them to fly. And what human can claim as many different designs as the God who created not only vultures, but bald eagles, ruby-throated hummingbirds, ring-necked pheasants, blue birds, great blue herons, and thousands of other awesome and beautiful species?

# Respect for Sharks

One morning, when I lived in Florida, some friends and I were water skiing in Biscayne Bay. The air was dead calm and, as we looked out toward the ocean, we could see that the water was as smooth as glass. So we skied right out into the ocean. Once out in the open sea it seemed that anything that could go wrong, did. One thing after another caused the skiers to drop into the water. Someone shouting from an incoming fishing boat reminded us that "there are sharks out here." The reminder should not have been necessary. We knew that there were sharks out there.

I can recall being on a fishing boat in those waters when someone had a really big one on his line. After a very long fight he brought it to the surface and the captain shot it with a shotgun. It was about twelve feet long.

We had all been to one or more of the aquariums where tourists go to see the sharks. We had all viewed these fearsome streamlined creatures which are designed so that they must swim constantly to stay alive. We had witnessed the frenzy at feeding time. We had watched in awe as they tore apart huge chunks of meat with their double rows of razor sharp teeth. And we knew the water we were in was inhabited by these swift and powerful giants. The warning should not have been necessary, but it was. We got everyone back into the boat and headed back to the relative safety of the bay. The One who created these amazing creatures also gave man enough intelligence to stay away from them.

# Cheeseburger Bird

While I was in my backyard one day, a particularly beautiful bird call caught my attention. In a rich melodious voice this bird was calling out what sounded to me like, "Cheeseburger, cheeseburger." I tried to locate the bird I was hearing, but could not see it. After that I would often hear the call and stop what I was doing to peer into the trees, hoping to identify the source of this cheerful song. I would see birds, but was unable to tell which one was calling "Cheeseburger." I whistled the call to other bird watchers, but no one recognized it. For years I knew this bird only as the cheeseburger bird.

Then one day I heard the clear ringing notes again. When I looked up, there he was perched on a branch right in front of me. I could see his head and beak move as he sang out, "Cheeseburger, cheeseburger." There was no doubt. This was definitely the bird I had been looking for. But to my surprise, it was a common ordinary blue jay—a blue jay, which I regarded as a nuisance, a noise maker, a big bully that chases the nice birds away. I didn't know he had any calls other than the raucous, "Jay, jay." According to the National Audubon Society, blue jays actually have a rich variety of calls.

Almost immediately my attitude toward the blue jays began to change. I no longer think of them as a nuisance. I even admire their beautiful blue color with black and white markings. I wonder, if it was so easy to change my attitude toward blue jays, why is it so hard to change our attitudes toward people of other ethnic groups?

# Saga of the Elk

The American elk once roamed the countryside over most of what is now the United States. They were called *wapiti* by the Shawnee Indians. Then white men came and took over the area. Hunters killed so many elk that they survived only in the area west of the Rockies. Now elk have been brought back to several regions which were once their native homeland.

I have occasionally visited the elk viewing area in Pennsylvania. What an experience it is to see these wild animals with their impressive antlers. Oftentimes they can be seen grazing close to roads and buildings, seemingly unconcerned about the presence of humans. I've seen groups of five or more large bulls grazing peacefully in lawns on the edge of the town.

I find satisfaction in knowing that we are helping these magnificent animals to survive. We are certainly doing the right thing. In the long run, I wonder who suffered more at the hands of us white newcomers, the elk or the Native Americans who called them *wapiti*.

# Precision Performance Animals

Dolphins and bats have been using a form of sonar called echo-location since long before man developed the technology. They emit a series of high-pitched sounds and listen for the echoes coming back from objects around them. This helps them to navigate and locate their prey.

Also, dolphins and bats are both known for their precision maneuvers. Many dolphins have been trained to perform precise jumps and acrobatic routines. As bats fly about in the evening feeding on insects, their quick turns and sudden dives make them interesting to watch.

A friend of mine tells of being in a room where there was an exhaust fan with no guard on the inside or outside. While the fan was running, a bat entered the room through the fan without hitting a blade. It flew around the room a few times and then exited through the fan, again avoiding a collision with the revolving blades.

I've seen a lot of precision maneuvers by the Blue Angels and other stunt pilots. I am certainly entertained and amazed at their performances. But with a stunt like flying through a fan, I would say that bats are one up on humans.

# Changing Seasons

Almost everyone enjoys touring the countryside in the autumn when the hills are ablaze with color. As the trees turn their vibrant greens to endless shades of red and gold they create a spectacular outdoor environment for man to enjoy. They remind us of the upcoming hunting seasons and Thanksgiving. They warn us of the approaching winter. But in a short time the glorious colors fade and the leaves drop to the ground.

As they decay, the leaves put humus and nutrients back into the soil. These nutrients will be used by future plants, thus continuing the cycle of life, death and life. This is only one of the many different cycles that enable the earth's ecosystems to continue functioning. There is the cycle of rivers flowing to the sea where the water evaporates and returns to the earth as rain or snow. There is the cycle of oxygen and carbon dioxide. There is also the cycle of the changing seasons as the earth orbits the sun.

I am reminded of a song that was popular in the sixties.

> *To everything—*
>     *Turn, turn, turn,*
> *There is a season—*
>     *Turn, turn, turn,*
> *And a time to every purpose under heaven.*
> *A time to be born,*
> *A time to die; ...*

The rest of the lyrics can be found in the Bible, in Ecclesiastes, chapter 3, verses 1-8.

# Lean Toward the Rock

Most of us who do down-river canoeing, at some time find ourselves being swept broadside toward a rock. You see it coming, you try to maneuver around it. But it's too little, too late. You know you're going to hit. Our natural reaction is to lean away from the rock. That's a reaction based on fear and it only makes the problem worse.

When you lean away from the rock, the upstream side of the canoe will be deep in the water and the downstream side will be high. As the boat strikes the rock the downstream side will be pushed even higher, forcing the upstream side deeper into the water. As the boat stops, the current catches the upstream edge and pulls it under. The boat capsizes with the open top facing the current. In this position the moving water can create tons of pressure pinning the canoe against the rock and sometimes wrapping the canoe around the rock.

On the other hand, if you lean downstream when you see a collision coming, the upstream side of the canoe will be high. As the boat stops against the rock, the current will be forced under the boat, raising it up and helping to free it from the rock. So when you see you can't avoid hitting a rock, don't react in fear. Lean toward the rock.

When you need to go through adversity in life, face it bravely. Fear usually makes things worse. In the Bible, James tells us to consider it joy when we face trials, because this helps us develop perseverance. Franklin Roosevelt said, "The only thing we have to fear is fear itself." The twenty-third Psalm says, "I will fear no evil, for you are with me." Lean toward the rock.

# A Bluefish's Revenge

It's always exciting to catch a bluefish. Even a small one can give you quite a fight. I'll never forget one of my first bluefish. After fighting the fish to the surface, I hoisted it into the boat and let it down on the deck. With one hand I picked up the pliers to remove the hook. With the other hand I reached down to grasp the line about ten inches above the fish. At that instant he slapped his tail against the deck and heaved his head upward. With one snap of his jaw he lacerated my thumb from one end to the other.

The injury was not serious enough to bring the boat in early. The mate got out the first aid kit and we bandaged the wound. I continued to fish the rest of the day, but with a throbbing pain in my thumb. Of course, as I fished, my bandage eventually became soaked with salt water which naturally made the pain even worse. I had an enjoyable day catching bluefish, although the pain kept reminding me that something was wrong.

No one appreciates pain at the time. But it is another one of nature's marvelous little devices helping us to survive. When I got home I went directly to my doctor and got proper medical treatment.

# Pain

Although pain is one of nature's devices intended to help us, sometimes pain may become so intense that it prevents us from doing the things we need to do to regain our health. On a weekend trip to the mountains I developed an extremely painful sore throat. On Friday I was able to enjoy some hiking and bird-watching. But eating was not enjoyable at all. By Saturday afternoon I could no longer swallow any solid food. That night I almost choked trying to swallow a dose of medicine. I dreaded doing any kind of oral hygiene. Pain had become my enemy instead of my friend.

On Monday I was finally able to get to a doctor and was diagnosed with herpes and strep-throat. After several more days of excruciating pain, I slowly regained my health. I hope I never have to endure pain like that again.

During this painful ordeal, I occasionally meditated on the horrendous pain that Christ suffered for me. After being severely beaten and whipped, and having His beard pulled out and a crown of thorns pressed onto His head, He allowed them to drive spikes through His hands and feet. He willingly accepted this as the punishment for our sins. Then the weight of His body hung on those spikes till He died. I'm sure my sore throat was nothing compared to the pain of crucifixion. My mind cannot comprehend the amount of pain He suffered. But I can appreciate it a little more than I did before.

# Hunting Duo

There are many species of animals that kill others for food. Some will kill when provoked or threatened, but only a few will kill for sport. Two of these are dogs and man. No wonder we have become best friends. Most experts believe that man is the more intelligent of this hunting duo, although some may question this at times. If we are the more intelligent, then it is our responsibility to see that this hunting instinct is used to help rather than hurt mother nature. Wildlife management and the sport of hunting have come a long way since the days when Buffalo Bill and others slaughtered the American bison. Now the hunter plays an important role in managing herd sizes and preventing mass starvation. We have come to realize the lasting impact we have on our environment. We value every species.

If you believe, as I do, that our environment is a gift from the Creator, then it is a unique treasure to be cared for and passed on to future generations. However, if you believe that all this came about randomly, then our environment is even more unique and it is paramount that we preserve it. The Almighty God could create another earth just as magnificent as this one. But if all this evolved by chance, odds are that will never happen again in all eternity. Odds are it didn't happen by chance the first time.

# Urban and Rural Wildlife

One place I frequently go canoeing is the West Branch of the Susquehanna River as it winds through the mountains of northern Pennsylvania. It is a beautiful area. There are a few cabins here and there, a railroad with a tunnel, but other than that it is pretty much wilderness. Oftentimes the water is clear enough to allow a good view of the river bottom.

Another place I go is an urban area on the Schuylkill River as it skirts around the edge of the city of Reading. The water is usually cloudy. I pass a sewage treatment plant and there are more upstream. At some places industrial buildings come right up to the edge of the water. There are numerous bridges and highways, remains of old canal locks and city parks. There is always a variety of floating and submerged junk from civilization.

Ironically, I always see more wildlife on the urban trip than I do in the mountains. Along the Schuylkill I usually see kingfishers and great blue herons. Osprey are not uncommon and geese are always in the area. Those rare times when the water is clear enough, I may even see schools of fish. I see none of these things on my Susquehanna trip, although once we were fortunate enough to have a black bear swim across the river in front of us. You see, run-off from coal mines has polluted this section of the Susquehanna. Sulfur from the mines combines with the oxygen in the water forming sulfur dioxide, thus removing the oxygen and making it impossible for fish to live. Since there are no fish there are no fish-eating birds.

Recent efforts to clean up this pollution seem to be paying off and fish are gradually coming back to this section of the river. I am encouraged by seeing past mistakes corrected. I am also delighted to see wildlife flourishing so near a busy urban area. It shows we can live in harmony with nature.

# The Plight of Snakes

I think snakes are victims of a lot of prejudice. Most snakes do no harm to humans nor to our possessions. In fact they help us by eating a lot of harmful and pesky rodents. So why do we hate them so much? Now I know a few species are poisonous. But there are also many other types of creatures that are dangerous and more aggressive than snakes. They are not despised as much as snakes are. Take bears for instance. Most of us enjoy watching bears. Some people even feed them and try to get close to them. Occasionally someone is injured or killed and many cars and campers are damaged by bears trying to get to food. Yet we love bears. More people are killed by bee stings than snake bites. Ticks and mosquitoes carry life-threatening diseases, but do they alarm us the way snakes do? Are the stripes on a tiger more appealing than the stripes on a garter snake? The tiger is certainly much more dangerous. Are we frightened by the way a snake slides smoothly along with almost undetectable motion then suddenly strikes its victim? We admire the stealthiness of cougars and other large cats. We do not dislike them the way we do snakes. I know there are a few people, like myself, who don't hate snakes and don't really love them either. There are even fewer who think snakes make nice pets. Most of us have very little appreciation for these colorful and helpful creatures. Maybe we're insulted because they stick their tongues out at us. However, I believe it is generally known that they use their tongues to sense odors. So they are not insulting us, they're just checking if we stink.

I really don't know why snakes are so unpopular. Maybe the answer is found in the Bible. In the third chapter of Genesis God cursed the serpent and said that He would put enmity between the offspring of the woman and the offspring of the serpent. Six thousand years later there still seems to be plenty of enmity.

# Nothing New Under the Sun

In 1942 a group of scientists produced the first man-made nuclear chain reaction, paving the way for the development of atomic bombs and nuclear power plants. In the decades that followed, the United States and Russia raced to develop this tremendous new power. Three thousand years earlier, the wise King Solomon had written, "There is nothing new under the sun." Solomon was right, of course. Even nuclear energy is not new. The sun itself is a thermonuclear reaction which was going on long before Solomon was born.

Ever since the dawn of creation, the sun has been spewing out nuclear energy in the form of heat, visible light, ultraviolet rays and other types of radiation. Only about two-billionth of the sun's radiation comes in the direction of our planet, and the earth's atmosphere partially protects us from the harmful effects. Somehow the earth receives just the right amount of the sun's energy for living things to survive here.

For years there has been much concern about contaminating our environment with radioactive materials. These concerns have increased greatly since the nuclear accidents at Three Mile Island and Chernobyl. We should be concerned about this and do all we can to protect ourselves and our environment. I find it ironic, however, that people worry about radiation from a controlled fission reaction inside a pressure vessel, inside a containment building, and yet they will lie out on the beach and expose themselves to the thermonuclear fusion reaction in the sky. Maybe if we started thinking of the sun as a nuclear reactor we would be more careful to protect ourselves from it.

*Gazing at the scenery in the Swiss Alps.*

# Hiking the Swiss Alps

The most beautiful place I have ever hiked was in the Swiss Alps in the area around Grindelwald. Vacationing there with my family, we took a number of one-day hikes through the scenic countryside. It was summer and the farmers were mowing and raking hay on slopes too steep for normal farm equipment.

Much of the work was done by hand. There was constant music of cowbells from the herds grazing around us. From the mountain top we could look down on a beautiful patchwork of fields and forest with tiny chalets and farm buildings scattered about. We could stop almost anywhere and gaze across the valley at several rugged rocky peaks with glaciers wedged between them. In the distance we could see even larger snow-capped mountains. Wild flowers were blooming in abundance. Every house had flower beds and window boxes filled with colorful flowers. Streams of crystal clear water gurgled down the slopes gathering together into raging torrents in the valleys. Words can hardly describe the beauty of this place.

As I hiked, a song kept ringing through my mind. It was a song written by Dottie Rambo. I had heard it sung at my uncle's funeral just before leaving for vacation.

> *The holy hills of heaven call me*
> *To mansions bright across the sea,*
> *Where loved ones wait and crowns are given -*
> *The hills of home keep calling me.*
> *This house of flesh is but a prison!*
> *Bars of bone hold my soul;*
> *But the doors of clay are gonna burst wide open*
> *When the angels set my spirit free;*
> *I'll take my flight like the mighty eagle,*
> *When the hills of home start calling me.*

# Life in the Ant Colony

It was a quiet evening and the air was dead calm. Suddenly there was a loud crack as a twelve-inch-diameter branch broke loose from the top of a wild cherry tree next to our house. It came crashing down, ripping electric wires, phone wires, and the electric meter off the side of the house. The cause—carpenter ants. High up in the tree these little culprits had been busy expanding their living quarters with no concern for the structural integrity of their renovation.

Ants are industrious little creatures and able to carry many times their own weight. It seems they are always busy gathering food or building their nests. But they are unable to think and plan as we do. They just scurry about doing whatever comes natural for ants. Some kinds of ants keep livestock in the form of aphids and leafhoppers. These insects produce a liquid called honeydew on which the ants can feed. Leafcutter ants take pieces of leaves and flowers into their nests and use it to make a damp mash on which mushrooms will grow. The ants then eat the mushrooms. Ants do not think about why they do these things. I doubt that they ever stop to admire their accomplishments, even when they have done something significant like bringing down electric lines. I don't suppose they ever receive compliments or praise from their companions. I've never heard of them taking time to relax and have fun. They just work.

John Lennon, in one of his songs, asks us to imagine there's no heaven, no hell, no countries, no religion, and no possessions. He presents this as if it would be some sort of utopia. To me it sounds more like a colony of ants. Ants have no religion, no possessions, and no eternal destiny. Like Lennon however, I too look for a future time when the world will live as one. I expect this to happen when the Almighty Creator and Savior returns from heaven to be the supreme ruler of all countries. The forces of evil will be banished to hell and all creatures will share the rich bounty of the earth. We are much more than an ant colony.

# How Do
# Butterflies Navigate?

The migration of birds is amazing. However, I find the migration of butterflies much more amazing. How can such delicate little insects fly thousands of miles and cross large bodies of water? The monarch butterfly migrates from North America across the Gulf of Mexico to Central America and back again. The painted lady migrates from Europe across the Mediterranean Sea to Africa and back again. How can these little creatures, who have never had any contact with their parents, find their way to a place they have never been? I have read that some monarchs fly to the very same trees that their ancestors had migrated to previously. How do they do that? I consider myself a bit smarter than a butterfly yet I sometimes have trouble finding my destination with the help of a map and written directions.

Did the Creator program the directions for migration into their tiny brains? Did he give them some type of global positioning technology not yet discovered by man? Or do they receive guidance directly from the Creator? I haven't a clue. The Bible does tell us that God cares for the little things of His creation. It also says that He places a much higher value on you and me.

# A Dove and a Hawk

When I came home from work one afternoon I walked to my patio door and noticed a coopers hawk and a mourning dove resting peacefully side by side. They were not perching as birds usually do. They were lying on their backs with their feet sticking up in the air. It was a comical sight but the scenario that had evidently taken place had been quite serious. Apparently the hawk was looking for a meal. The dove was trying to avoid becoming that meal. Both were doing what they had to do to survive. Flying as fast as they could in a life-and-death race, they both flew headlong into an unforeseen obstacle, my patio door. Now they lay side by side, only inches apart, with their feet sticking up in the air.

Like the birds, we all get caught up in a race, a struggle to get ahead or stay ahead of others. Like the birds, we can't see all the obstacles in our path. Unlike the birds, we have the ability to contemplate death and what happens after death. For thousands of years, people of many different religions have believed that there is life after death, and that things done in this life affect our next life. I can't prove that they are all wrong, so to be on the safe side I'm assuming that at least some of them are right. The hawk and dove on my patio reminded me that my life here could end as abruptly and unexpectedly as theirs. So then, how should we prepare for the future?

# Dress for Success

On a cool drizzly morning in early spring, Jim and I set out on the Schuylkill River. Our objective was to water test Jim's new canoe and some of the gear and clothing we were collecting for a seven-day wilderness trip we were planning for later that spring. We were wearing items of wool, acrylic, polypropylene and similar materials. On top we wore nylon rain suits.

The river was running strong from the recent rains. As we approached the rapids at Kelly's Lock we could see huge standing waves waiting for us. We started in slowly. We rode over the first wave and plunged into the second. As the boat came out of the second wave it tipped over and threw us into the drink. We weren't trying to capsize, but we knew that was what we needed to completely test our gear.

Within seconds the frigid water flooded into my rain suit, from the bottom upward. The initial shock of cold water hitting my body made me gasp, as it always does. But the discomfort did not last long. We drifted with the current for a little while, expecting it to bring us into a shallow area. But on this day, that shallow area did not exist.

Before we started our swim for shore, we both commented that we were no longer feeling very cold. By the time we got to shore and hauled in our boat and gear, we both felt warm enough that we thought it unnecessary to change our clothing. We could change later if we found we were unable to stay warm. For the time it seemed better to keep our dry clothes dry. Although the weather was rather chilly, we canoed another three hours to our take-out, wearing our wet clothes and feeling quite comfortable, and a little more cautious.

Wearing the right clothes can make all the difference. For this kind of sport you need clothes that will keep you warm even when wet. That means they must be made of fabrics that do not absorb very much water. An outer layer of something like nylon helps to keep the cool air from coming in contact with the wet layers underneath. In severe conditions a wet suit or a dry suit should be worn.

You never know what challenges a day of canoeing will bring. The time to prepare is before the need arises. Be sure you are dressed properly before you get on the river. One who goes unprepared is like the person who waits for his death bed before preparing for eternity. There is no guarantee that he'll get that chance.

# Beware of Dams

It's always an adventure when you get into a canoe and explore an unfamiliar river. As you make your way downstream, you must be on the lookout for the unknown dangers you may encounter. You never know what you may find around the next bend. On one such excursion, my brother and I were looking downstream, a bit confused about where the river was leading us. We couldn't tell if the next bend went to the left or the right. Soon we realized that the river did not go to the left or to the right. It went straight down! We hurried to the shore and portaged around a twenty-foot high dam. It was hard to believe that we could be so close to such a large dam and not be able to see it. But that is not unusual.

Many dams are almost impossible to see as you approach from upstream. With your eyes only three to four feet above the water, the flat water above the dam may blend into the downstream landscape in a way that is very deceptive. You may be only a few yards from the dam-breast and still have the impression that there is a great expanse of flat water ahead of you.

Of course, the sensible thing to do would be to go with someone who is familiar with the river and knows where such hazards lie. Another option is to read guide books and study topographical maps. It's really quite foolish to embark on a river with no knowledge of what lies ahead.

Life itself is an adventure. We never know what we will encounter around the next bend. Many things in our environment are beyond our control. We can, however, put our trust in the One who knows the future. We can study His guide book, the Bible. I wouldn't want to navigate through life without His help.

# Rattlesnake for Dinner

A friend of mine invited me along on a backpacking trip. He was taking a group of teenage boys on a weekend hike on the Black Forest Trail in northern Pennsylvania. After a day of hiking we chose a site and set up our camp. A few yards from our campsite we killed a large rattlesnake. While lounging around the camp after dinner, a few of the boys got the notion that we should roast the rattlesnake and eat it. Several hours after we had killed and decapitated it, they retrieved the snake's body, which was still wiggling. They gutted it and skinned it. We cut a straight slender branch from a tree and tied it along the length of the snake. We basted it with butter and held it over the fire. The meat was white like crab meat and the flavor was somewhere between crab and chicken. Everyone in the group at least tasted it. Some of us thought it was quite good while others just couldn't get past the repulsive idea of eating a snake.

This earth has so many delicious foods to offer us. We can enjoy lobster and steak, shrimp, veal, baked potatoes with sour cream, bacon and eggs, peaches, pineapples, strawberries, barbecued chicken, hot peppers, sugar peas, watermelons, mushrooms, scallops, fish, apples, oranges, and whatever else you'd like to put on the list. With so many excellent choices, I guess I won't criticize anyone if he doesn't want rattlesnake on the menu. But, it really is good.

# The Good and the Ugly

It was one of those days with a clear blue sky and bright sunshine that beg you to do something outdoors. I was out with my super 8-mm camera filming the Florida landscape when I came upon a beautiful scene by a small canal with palm trees and tropical plants. There was one problem, however. The water had an ugly dark brown color. Everything else was so fresh, clean looking and picturesque. So I decided to shoot some film in spite of the nasty-looking water.

When I got the film developed I was surprised to see that the camera had captured something I had missed completely. In the water was a beautiful reflection of blue sky, green plants and palm trees. The colors in the reflection were so strong that you couldn't tell the actual color of the water.

I wonder how many times I miss something pleasant and wonderful because my attention is focused on something ugly.

# Morning Music

I'm not exactly a morning person. I like to sleep in when I have a chance. On camping trips I'm usually not the first one out of my sleeping bag. But when I do get up early, I find the morning a very delightful and inspiring time of day. It's always uplifting to watch the sunrise and to see the morning mist rising from a lake or a river. It's always stimulating to see the dew sparkling in the morning sun and hear the birds singing so cheerfully.

I love to sing that song, "Morning Has Broken," written by Eleanor Farjeon.

*Morning has broken*
*Like the first morning,*
*Blackbird has spoken*
*Like the first bird.*
*Praise for the singing!*
*Praise for the morning!*
*Praise for them springing*
*Fresh from the Word!*

*Sweet the rain's new fall*
*Sunlit from heaven,*
*Like the first dew-fall*
*On the first grass.*
*Praise for the sweetness*
*Of the wet garden,*
*Sprung in completeness*
*Where His feet pass.*

*Mine is the sunlight!*
*Mine is the morning,*
*Born of the one light*
*Eden saw play!*
*Praise with elation,*
*Praise every morning,*
*God's re-creation*
*Of the new day!*

# Going the Long Hard Way

One morning on a canoe camping trip along the Allagash Wilderness Waterway we looked across a peaceful Chamberlain Lake. As we left our campsite at Lost Spring we headed diagonally across the lake toward a point we could see protruding from the opposite shore. Just beyond the point we were to find Lock Dam where we would make a short portage. As we paddled across the open water a slight head wind picked up, giving us a bit of chop and slowing our progress. About three fourths of the way across we crossed paths with another group of canoeists. We exchanged a few words and discovered that although our courses intersected at right angles we all had the same destination, Lock Dam. They continued on their course and we continued on ours. After paddling long and hard against the wind, we reached the point and rounded the bend. We paddled along the shore till we came to Chamberlain Farm. It was only then that we realized that we were four miles beyond Lock Dam. We turned our backs to the wind and had a much easier paddle back to our destination. If only we had checked our compass before leaving our campsite we would have realized that we were looking at the wrong point. We would have saved a lot of time and energy.

All of us need a good compass to keep our lives on the right course. What do you use to help you make ethical business decisions, to maintain healthy relationships, and choose wholesome social and recreational activities?

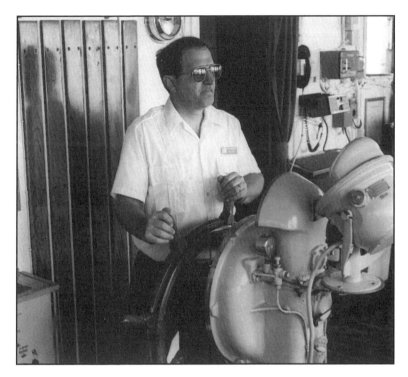

*Author at the helm of* Caribbean Mercy, *a hospital ship operated by Mercy Ships.*

# Chasing the Compass

As I took the helm of the ship, the officer in charge of my watch instructed me to steer 154 degrees. I watched the compass turn slowly to the right; 153 degrees, 152 degrees, 151 degrees. Which way do I turn the helm?

As I watch the compass turning to the right, my tendency is to turn the helm to the left. If I did that, however, the ship would turn farther to port and the compass would turn farther to the right. This common mistake is known as chasing the compass. So I turn the helm to the right, giving the rudder about five degrees. I hold the helm and wait. A 265-foot ship doesn't respond as quickly as the 16-foot canoe I am used to. Eventually the ship begins turning slowly to starboard and I see the compass coming back to my intended heading of 154 degrees. Of course, it doesn't stop there. The ship continues turning and veers off to starboard. So it takes continual working at the helm to keep the ship on course.

As the ship veers off course in one direction after the other, I feel no sensation that I am turning. As I look around the bridge, nothing around me appears to be changing its direction of travel. The only thing that appears to be turning is the dial of the compass. However, the truth is that the compass is the only thing that is not turning. The compass remains in a fixed direction as the ship and everything on board rotate to the left and then to the right.

As we move along with society around us, we may be veering off course to the left or to the right, and not realizing it. We may think that our guiding principles such as the Ten Commandments and the Golden Rule have become old-fashioned or irrelevant. The truth is these rules have not changed. The Golden Rule and the Ten Commandments are as good and valid as they ever were. If we think they have become irrelevant, it can only mean that we are about to turn the helm the wrong way and veer farther off course.

# Against the Current

I've canoed with groups of amateur canoeists and with groups of experienced white-water enthusiasts. One difference I notice is that the amateurs usually go faster. They have a tendency to point their boats downstream and paddle as if the water isn't moving fast enough. On the contrary, the more experienced boaters frequently turn their boats upstream and play in the currents. They stop in the eddies to rest or regroup. They ferry from eddy to eddy as they explore the whole river. They take time to test their skills against the rapids or to surf on a wave. It seems they want to stay on the water as long as possible while the amateurs rush toward their take-out point.

On the river of life we have the same kind of choices. We can allow ourselves to be swept along with the current and do what everyone else does. Or, we can turn our bow into the current and choose our own course. Are you taking time to paddle against the currents that try to control your life? Have you stopped in the eddies to appreciate all the wonderful things the Creator has put here for us? Have you thanked Him lately? Or are you one of those just rushing toward the end?

# The Power of a Hurricane

Several times each year mother nature displays her immeasurable power by sending a hurricane to the eastern United States or Central America. These huge storms with their powerful winds, heavy rain, and storm surge can leave a wide path of destruction hundreds of miles long. I've been to a number of disaster areas to help with the clean-up and rebuilding. I have seen the utter devastation they can cause. I have heard the almost unbelievable stories of the survivors. To call these storms awesome is an understatement. My mind can not comprehend the amount of energy released by a hurricane.

It all begins with a gentle updraft as air is warmed by the waters of the Atlantic Ocean. This creates a low pressure center. Air being drawn into the center from surrounding areas is also warmed and rises continually drawing in more air. As the earth rotates, the air, land, sea and low pressure center all move toward the east, but the things closer to the equator are moving faster than things closer to the poles. So as air from the south is drawn northward it gets ahead of the low pressure center and misses the center to the east. Likewise, the air coming down from the north is moving too slowly and falls behind, missing the center to the west. As the northern and southern winds miss on opposite sides they spiral toward the center, starting the counter-clockwise rotation typical of all hurricanes in the northern hemisphere. The faster the wind swirls the lower the pressure drops. As the pressure drops the storm intensifies. As long as warm waters fuel the updrafts the storm grows in size and/or strength.

Hurricanes can make us realize how small and powerless we are. They remind us how much we rely on others and on God. Just ask those who have faced the fury of these powerful storms.

# Flotilla Fellowship

Some canoe safety advisors recommend canoeing in groups of not less than three boats. While this may not always be necessary, it is good advice. The more boats in the group, the more resources you have to respond to an emergency. The more people in the group, the more they can help each other, provided they have the required skills. When one canoe capsizes, others are there to assist if needed. When running difficult rapids, someone can stand by with a rescue line. If someone is injured, friends can administer first aid and help to get him to a medical facility if necessary. Those with more experience can advise and assist those with less experience. Those who go ahead can give direction to those who are following.

Additionally, what could be more fun than canoeing with a group when all are interested in the same sport that you are? All of us enjoy being with others who share our interests.

As we navigate through life, all of us need to be part of a group. We need to help each other through difficult times. We need to get advice and direction from others. We need fellowship with others who share our values and goals. What could be better than that?

# Man's Best Friend

Dogs have often been called man's best friend and there is good reason for that. There seems to be a special bond between humans and dogs in spite of the fact that dogs are attracted to some things that we find quite repulsive. They seem to enjoy sniffing around at anything with a bad odor. They may roll themselves on a decaying carcass or other rotting material which we wouldn't even touch. We can bathe them with shampoo and give them a smell more pleasing to ourselves. We can prevent them from eating what we consider unhealthy. We may even be able to teach them not to drink from the toilet. But we can't change their nature. They will still be attracted to things we recognize as filthy. None the less, we love dogs and they love us.

This reminds me that God loves me even though I, by my nature, am attracted to things that are offensive to Him. In the Bible, He has given us instructions on how He wants us to live. These instructions are for our benefit, not His. But He understands our sinful nature and He knows we are not capable of living up to all His commandments. In spite of all our failures, He still loves us much more than any man could love a dog. He loves us so much that He sent His only son to die for our sins and restore our relationship with Him. How could I not love Him?

# Two Kinds of Dogs

Some dogs seem to be always eager to do things for their master. Whether it be trailing a rabbit or jumping into a lake to retrieve a stick, they will do whatever he asks. They love to catch a Frisbee or play tug-of -war with an old sock. They always want to be near their master and interacting with him in some way. Other dogs seem intent on getting away from their owners and pursuing their own interests. They constantly strain at their leashes. These dogs must be kept on leashes or they will run off and get into trouble.

Which kind of dog would you like to be? I would like to be the kind that wags its tail with eager anticipation whenever it sees the Master. I would be one that runs to meet Him and walks by His side. I want to trust my Master and rely on Him to supply all my needs. I want to live in the Master's house where He hands me food from His table. When He sits down to relax, I'll snuggle up beside Him and lay my head on His lap. I'll be so happy because He has forgotten the times I ran away and He did not disown me when I bit His son. When He rubs my ears and strokes my fur, I know He cares for me. In the evening, when it's time to sleep, I want to curl up at the Master's feet. What kind of dog do you want to be?

# Purple Trillium

On the sixth evening of a seven-day canoe trip in the Allagash Wilderness we stopped at a campsite at Round Pond. It was a very wet piece of land between the lake and a boggy area. All of us were tired from six days of paddling and wet from three days of rain. We were dirty and unshaven, but having a good time roughing it in the wilderness. Everyone was busy working around the campsite trying to make the best of our dreary conditions when someone called out, "Hey, look what I found." Six rugged males gathered around to admire a single flourishing stalk of purple trillium. It was the largest trillium I had ever seen and had two beautiful blossoms. I think I can honestly say that this lone stalk of purple trillium brightened the day for each one of us. No wonder the ladies cherish flowers so much.

Flowers do much more than attract insects which pollinate them, helping the plants to reproduce. Flowers do much more than provide nectar for hummingbirds and honeybees, enabling them to survive. Flowers lift our spirits when we are down and help us through difficult times. Flowers say, "I love you." Flowers bring much cheer to the hearts of humans, especially when we consider who sent them.

*Dale with the huge trout he caught in the Yellow Breeches.*

# Trout-Fishing Outlaws

My friend Larry, my brother Dale, and my son Keith accompanied me on a weekend canoe camping trip on the Yellow Breeches Creek. We took along a can of worms and a few fishing rods. Dale brought along a very small, almost a toy, rod and reel which he had bought for his little boy. While fishing with this little outfit, Dale hooked a huge trout. After a long fight and some boat maneuvering, we landed the fish successfully. Only then did we realize that we had nothing with which to measure a fish. Dale put it on the stringer and hung it over the side of his canoe, eager to measure it when we got home. Some time later, after scraping by some rocks in fast moving water, we discovered our trophy fish was missing from the stringer. I know the biggest one always gets away, but it doesn't usually happen after the fish is dead. We caught plenty of others to replace it, although none nearly as large. We had a stringer full of nice trout as we drifted slowly by a sign facing downstream. As we passed the sign we looked back to learn that the area we were leaving was restricted to fly fishing only and catch and release. Luckily we did not encounter any law enforcement and that evening we had a delicious meal of fresh trout cooked over an open campfire.

We had not intended to be law breakers, but ignorance is no excuse. We were guilty, even though we hadn't realized it while we were violating the law.

All of us are guilty of breaking God's laws from time to time. The difference is that God offers a full pardon to all who admit their guilt and accept His offer. It doesn't matter how serious the offense nor whether it was intentional or unintentional. There are no legal fees and no bribes to be paid. His pardon is completely free. How could I refuse such an offer?

# Difficult Decisions

One of my early canoe expeditions was a weekend canoe camping trip on the Lehigh River. My brother Dean and I scouted the area as well as we could from land. Although much of the river was inaccessible by road, what we could see looked pretty inviting. I was too ignorant to realize that this stretch of river contained a lot of class-three whitewater. I thought we were experienced canoeists and could handle anything this river had to offer. What a novice I really was! I invited along two of our cousins who were avid outdoorsmen but had virtually no canoeing experience.

On a rainy Saturday morning we headed down the Lehigh in two open canoes loaded with camping gear. We had no spray covers, no flotation bags, and no wet suits. Almost immediately we began to realize that this river was more than we had anticipated. Our progress was slow as we got hung up on one rock after another. We had to stop frequently to empty the water out of our boats or recover from a capsize.

Eventually, feeling that we might have made a big mistake, we stopped to talk with a guide on one of the rafting expeditions that kept passing us. He encouraged us to keep going and assured us that we would have an enjoyable time. An enjoyable time was what we had come for and we weren't ready to give up on that, so we took his advice and kept going. After all, we didn't want to give anyone a reason to call us chicken. We kept working our way down the river, but by mid-afternoon it was obvious that we would be very late getting to our take-out point, if we got there at all. After spending some time standing under an overhanging rock, watching a steady rain falling on the swollen river, we made a difficult decision. We would abort the trip and carry the canoes out. Looking back, it seems that decision should have been a no-brainer. In reality, it was anything but that.

Nearby we found a grassy area along the railroad track where we set up camp. We built a bonfire and got warmed up and dried out. After eating a good dinner we crawled into our sleeping bags and got some rest.

Sunday morning broke clear and sunny. After a healthy breakfast we packed our gear in the canoes. We built a skid to slide on the railroad track, put the canoes on the skid, harnessed ourselves to the skid and headed up the railroad. Occasionally we had to clear the tracks for a freight train to pass, but other than that we made steady progress. After hours of hard work, we finally came to a road. From here Dean hitch-hiked back to our truck at the put-in.

So we had an enjoyable weekend in the outdoors, got plenty of exercise, and arrived home safely. But only because we were able to make that difficult decision. I have rafted and canoed this section of river several times since that. Today park rangers patrol this area to make sure that all boats are properly equipped. I am totally convinced that our decision to turn around was absolutely the best thing we could have done.

Sooner or later we all find ourselves in a position where we need to turn our lives around and go in a different direction. It takes humility to admit that we were wrong. It takes a lot of courage to turn around and point your life in a new direction. It may take a lot of work to recover from the situation we have gotten into.

I recall a decision I made when I was about twelve years old. I was sitting under a big tent, listening to an evangelist. I don't remember what he preached about, but I remember the banner that hung above him. It had the words of Jesus, "Ye must be born again." The word "must" kept hitting me like the beacon from a lighthouse. I knew I had to turn my life around or I would end up in hell. It should have been an easy decision, but it wasn't. Tears trickled down my face as I walked down the isle and accepted Christ as my savior. I know I made the right choice and I have never regretted it.

# Helter-skelter Squirrels

Why do squirrels get killed on the road? Their eyesight and sense of hearing are easily good enough to detect an approaching vehicle while it is still a safe distance away. They can run fast enough to clear several traffic lanes in a flash. Yet they die on the road. The problem seems to be that squirrels are not very good at making decisions. They run one way then the other, continually changing their minds. They may be more than three-fourths of the way across the road and decide to turn back. They keep changing their mind until disaster overtakes them.

In the same way many people are headed for eternal punishment because they never make the decision to follow Christ and accept the forgiveness He offers. They have heard about heaven and hell. They have heard that Christ died to forgive their sins. They can see that death will eventually overtake them. But, like the squirrels, they can't seem to decide which way to go. How tragic.

# Why I Wear My Life Jacket

When I first started canoeing I didn't wear a life jacket unless conditions appeared rather dangerous. Most of the time my life jacket just lay in the bottom of my boat. As I gained more experience I began to realize that accidents can happen any time and anywhere. They often happen when you least expect it. As I gained experience in reading the water I learned that many hazards are very difficult or impossible to see as you approach from upstream. Looking back on what you just passed, it's easy to see the dangers, but it's not very easy to see what lies ahead. So I began wearing a life jacket faithfully whenever I go canoeing. I no longer need to decide when to put it on or take it off. I just keep it on and I have the comfort of knowing that I'll be safe even if I fall out of my boat. And, yes, that still happens.

This reminds me of the plan of salvation God has provided for us. He provides this freely to anyone who will accept it. I can let it lie in the bottom of my boat or I can accept it and put it on. I have put it on and I keep it on. It gives me the comfort of knowing that my soul is safe even when I fall into sin. And, yes, that still happens.

# Feeding Raccoons

One day we discovered two young raccoons on our porch. They soon scurried off into the woods and took refuge in my wood shed. I took some food out to them and coaxed them to take some of it right out of my hand. I'm not sure why I did that. Although this was before rabies had become so common in our area, I was still taking a chance of being bitten. People have coaxed many kinds of animals and birds to take food directly from them. Despite all the warnings, people continue to feed bears and other dangerous animals. There seems to be something in many of us that makes us want to get up close and friendly with the wild creatures. Of course, the animals don't understand that. They are only interested in the food. That's what makes it so dangerous and sometimes deadly.

I look forward to a time, predicted in the Bible, when all creatures will live together in harmony. They will no longer eat one another. The lion will lie down with the lamb, and a child will lead them. What a wonderful time that will be for those of us who love animals.

*A favorite campsite of the author.* Sketched by the author.

# My Campsite

When I go backpacking or canoe camping, I usually stay only one night at a campsite. So it doesn't have to be perfect. I like a campsite that's free of litter, not too muddy and not too rocky. I prefer a level area for my tent and a safe place for a campfire. But it doesn't have to be perfect, I'm only staying one night. I'll make myself content with whatever I can find. I'll improve the things I can, like pick up litter or gather stones for a fire ring. The next day I'll move on, leaving the place as clean and natural looking as I can. I want others, who will camp there later, to appreciate the place as much as I did.

Near the end of an extended camping trip, I'm always eager to get home, take a hot shower and sleep in a comfortable bed. At home, I am more concerned about the quality of my accommodations. I want a comfortable sofa and chairs, and reliable heating and plumbing systems. I want all my electrical appliances to work properly. I want my walls neatly papered or painted. I want a nice lawn with flowers and shrubbery. But all this I will one day leave to those who will camp here later. My home on this earth is not my final destination. I am merely camping on this planet. I am looking forward to a home in Heaven, a spectacular place way beyond my imagination. Meanwhile, I will be content with the campsite I have chosen.

# Amazing Metamorphosis

While canoeing the West Branch of the Susquehanna River we stopped for lunch by the bridge at Rolling Stone. Here we encountered an assembly of hundreds of tiger swallowtail butterflies. I had never seen so many butterflies in one location. It was fascinating to watch as multitudes of these beautiful yellow and black butterflies soared and swooped and fluttered in the gentle breeze.

As a youngster I had collected and mounted a few butterflies. I never went very far with that hobby since I didn't own a butterfly net. It is quite a challenge to catch a butterfly without a net. Sometimes I captured milkweed caterpillars and fed them till they formed a chrysalis. Then I waited eagerly for them to hatch into beautiful orange and black monarch butterflies. What an amazing metamorphosis.

The caterpillars get no training on how to shed their skin and form a chrysalis. They have no instructions on how to unfurl and flatten their new wings. They don't take flying lessons. Somehow they just know how to do all these things. After a lifetime of crawling and eating leaves, I wonder what it's like to take that first flight in the air and take that first sip of nectar.

I expect that some day I will go through a similar transformation. I believe that when I get to Heaven I will have a new body, similar in some ways to the one I have now, but in some ways quite different. I really don't know what it will be like. But I suppose that, like the butterfly, I will know just what to do with it.

# Preferred Posture

Most canoes have seats, but experienced canoeists don't recommend that you sit on them. Rather, you should kneel with your knees spread apart, your feet under the seat and your buttocks resting against the front edge of the seat. I must point out that some canoe seats are too low for this to be done safely. Don't risk getting your leg trapped and not being able to get out when the boat capsizes. But whenever possible, the kneeling position gives you much better control of the canoe. First, it puts your weight a little lower so the boat is not as top heavy. Secondly, it makes it easier to control the side-to-side balancing of the boat. When the boat starts to tip, you can quickly press down with one knee or the other. This is much more effective than trying to shift your weight to one butt cheek while sitting on the seat. Third, it brings your arms and shoulders a little closer to the waterline, making your paddle strokes a little less strenuous.

Of course, kneeling is also the traditional posture for talking to God. I would recommend that you do that as well. While paddling our streams and rivers we get a glimpse of the magnificent world that God designed and created especially for humans. Think about the water and the air, the rocks and the soil, heat and light, gravity and inertia, plants and animals all designed to work together to form a habitat for mankind. I thank Him for this wonderful planet we call home. I thank Him for guiding me around obstacles and bringing me safely through the rough waters. I kneel to Him.

*Riding over the waves at Kelly's Lock on the Schuylkill River.*

# To Ride the Waves

When the pressures of life seem overwhelming or the pace is too rapid, it's then I need to find an eddy, turn 180 degrees and stop. I need to look around at the magnificent world our Creator has given us. I need to contemplate our balanced ecosystem where plants provide oxygen, food, fuel and shelter for the animal kingdom which returns carbon dioxide, nutrients and cultivation. If ever I doubt that there is a God, I need to look more closely at the things He created. When I consider the flytraps and the trees, or when I watch a vulture soaring in the breeze or a honeybee gathering nectar, I am reminded that this was planned by a very intelligent God. If ever I wonder whether God loves me, I need to look at a flower or watch a sunset and wait quietly for the stars to appear. I need to listen to that quiet voice inside of me. I need to contemplate what He did for me on the cross.

When I read the Bible, I am amazed at the wisdom in this book. In addition to telling us of God's love, it gives us guidance for life's conflicts, solutions for our social problems and hope in time of despair. It teaches us how to prevent diseases and helps us understand our natural desires. If 2,000 to 6,000 years ago mankind had this much wisdom without divine inspiration, then we are certainly evolving backwards.

God teaches us and reveals Himself to us through the Bible and through nature. He speaks to us through that inner voice He placed in our hearts. If we listen we find a source of all we really need.

When my strength is renewed and my confidence is restored, I push my bow into the current, lean downstream and peel out of the eddy. I rejoin the mainstream, ready to ride the waves and navigate around the rocks.